PLATFORM PAPERS

QUARTERLY ESSAYS ON THE PERFORMING ARTS FROM CURRENCY HOUSE

No. 55
May 2018

Platform Papers Partners

We acknowledge with gratitude our Partners in continuing support of Platform Papers and its mission to widen understanding of performing arts practice and encourage change when it is needed:

Neil Armfield, AO
Anita Luca Belgiorno-Nettis Foundation
Andrew Bovell
Jan Bowen, AM
Jane Bridge
Katharine Brisbane, AM
Elizabeth Butcher, AM
Penny Chapman
Robert Connolly
Dr Peter Cooke, AM
Sally Crawford
Wesley Enoch
Ian Enright
Ferrier Hodgson
Larry Galbraith
Tony Grierson
Wayne Harrison, AM
Campbell Hudson
Lindy Hume
Professors Bruce King and Denise Bradley, AC
Justice François Kunc
Peter Lee
Dr Richard Letts, AM
Peter Lowry, OAM and Carolyn Lowry, OAM
David Marr
Helen O'Neil
Martin Portus
Lesley Power
Professor William Purcell
Queensland Performing Arts Centre Trust
Geoffrey Rush, AC
Seaborn Broughton Walford Foundation
Caroline Sharpen, Creative Industries Consulting
Sky Foundation
Dr Merilyn Sleigh
Maisy Stapleton
Augusta Supple
Christopher Tooher
Caroline Verge
Rachel Ward, AM and Bryan Brown, AM
Kim Williams, AM
Professor Di Yerbury, AM

And we welcome our MAJOR CORPORATE SPONSOR FOR 2018

To them and to all subscribers and Friends of Currency House we extend our grateful thanks.

Platform Papers Readers' Forum

Readers' responses to our previous essays are posted on our website. Contributions to the conversation (250 to 2000 words) may be emailed to info@currencyhouse.org.au. The Editor welcomes opinion and criticism in the interest of healthy debate but reserves the right to monitor where necessary.

Platform Papers, quarterly essays on the performing arts, is published every February, May, August and November and is available through bookshops, by subscription and on line in paper or electronic version. For details see our website at www.currencyhouse.org.au.

ART, POLITICS, MONEY:

Revisiting Australia's cultural policy

DAVID THROSBY

ABOUT THE AUTHOR

DAVID THROSBY, AO, is a Distinguished Professor of Economics at Macquarie University, Sydney, internationally recognised for his research and writing on the economics of art and culture. He is a graduate of the University of Sydney and received his doctorate from the London School of Economics. His current research interests include the economic circumstances of creative artists, heritage economics, the creative industries, and the relationships between economic and cultural policy. He has published widely on these subjects, including *Economics and Culture* (2000) and *The Economics of Cultural Policy* (2010), now standard texts. In 2006 he was author of Platform Papers 7, *Does Australia Need a Cultural Policy?*

He is a past-president of the Association for Cultural Economics International (ACEI) and Foundation Chair of the National Association for the Visual Arts; sits on the editorial boards of journals including the *Journal of Cultural Economics* and the *International Journal of Cultural Policy*; and has served on the boards of the Museum of Contemporary Art, Sydney, The Australian Museum and the Copyright Agency Ltd. With others he has compiled several surveys for the Australia Council for the Arts on the economic influence on the arts and their workers. His current work includes an ongoing national survey of remote Indigenous artists, linked to the ongoing discussion about the sustainability of remote communities and the potential for linking economic and cultural development through the arts. He is also a team member of a series of projects, funded by the World Bank, in Jordan, Lebanon and Saudi Arabia, evaluating the economic, social and cultural aspects of investment in heritage rehabilitation in the historic cities of the Middle East.

Acknowledgements

Having worked extensively on cultural policy in recent years, especially in the preparation of my book *The Economics of Cultural Policy* (Cambridge University Press, 2010), I have accumulated an intellectual debt to so many scholars and policy wonks in the field that it is impossible to acknowledge them all. Likewise, in writing the present paper I have been able to access an enormous range of opinion and analysis relating to arts and cultural policy in Australia that has appeared in journals, periodicals, blogs and the press. I hesitate to mention names, but some contributors to the debate do keep recurring—frequent commentators whose writings have been particularly useful to me include Jo Caust, Alison Croggon, Steve Dow, Ben Eltham, Julian Meyrick, Justin O'Connor, Helen O'Neil, David Pledger, Julianne Schultz and many others. None of them can be held responsible for any of the views expressed herein. I apologise to any that I have inadvertently omitted. Gratitude is also due to the estimable publications in which much of their work has appeared—*The Conversation, The Monthly, Meanjin, Griffith Review* and of course *Platform Papers.* Apart from this general acknowledgement, there are several people whom I specifically want to thank. First, with the usual caveat, I express my gratitude to Katharine

Brisbane, John Senczuk and Nick Shimmin for their insightful comments on an earlier draft of this paper. Second, Hayley Megan French provided expert research assistance in helping me to locate a large number of sources and to take them on board. Finally, I owe an enormous debt of gratitude to Laura Billington in the Department of Economics at Macquarie University. Her consummate editorial skills always manage to turn my scribblings into coherent prose, and her commitment to the work makes it possible for me to meet otherwise impossible deadlines.

Introduction

In 2006 I wrote one of the early *Platform Papers* (No. 7) under the title *Does Australia Need a Cultural Policy?* I was prompted to ask this question because it was then twelve years since the appearance of Australia's first (and only) cultural policy, the document *Creative Nation: Commonwealth Cultural Policy* (October 1994) produced by the Keating Government. In the interim, following the Labor Party's defeat at the 1996 election, we experienced ten years of John Howard's prime ministership. Howard led a conservative administration that effectively buried *Creative Nation* when it came into office and subsequently showed no interest in formulating a cultural policy of its own.

A further reason for writing that paper was that Australia had undergone a period of profound economic and cultural change during a decade of Coalition rule. On the economic front, the Howard Government pursued policies of deregulation, privatisation and an inexorable transfer of power over resources from public to private hands; the values of individualism and materialism that were fundamental to the liberal economic project held centre stage. Howard was also a conservative in cultural terms, looking to Australia's past as inspiration for his vision of nationhood. He constantly referred to defining moments like Gallipoli and Kokoda as opportunities for the Australian battler to emerge as hero and the pivotal characteristics of mateship to be forged. These sorts of considerations informed his view of Australian identity, and as a result he regarded any debate about other notions of 'Australian-ness' or Australian culture as irrelevant.[1]

So I wrote the paper reflecting on these changes and concluded by answering my rhetorical question in the affirmative. Since then the ebb and flow of political fortunes have continued to affect the country, so that today it seems more than ever appropriate to ask the question once more. Do the arguments that were relevant in 2006 still apply today? What impacts have the changes in the economic, social and cultural landscape that have occurred in the intervening period had on policy towards the cultural sector?

In this paper I address these issues initially by revisiting the notion of a cultural policy, looking at the ways in which this concept has evolved in contemporary times. In particular, from my vantage point as an economist, I can reflect on the implications of what has been termed the 'economisation' of cultural policy that has been observed in the world at large over the last couple of decades. I then go on to consider the events and policy changes in Australia since 2006 that have affected the arts and culture under successive federal administrations. In a third section, I look in more detail at some major issues still unresolved, including the role of Indigenous arts, and the situation of the individual artist. Finally I draw some conclusions and make some recommendations on where we might go from here. In this paper I cast the net widely over areas of concern to cultural policy, but I have to confess in advance that I have not been able to deal adequately with two areas: the public broadcasters, and the film industry. While both of these areas are integral to Australian cultural policy, a proper treatment of them would require a whole paper, indeed several, for a full policy analysis.[2]

Before getting started, I reiterate below some of the conflicting facts about this country that I noted in summing up my 2006 paper and that led me to believe that a new cultural policy was needed at that time:[3]

- the Federal Government pledges its support for the arts, but is reluctant to provide the levels of funding that could catalyse a new renaissance in their production and consumption;
- the Prime Minister asserts that there is no need to discuss Australian identity, yet beats the patriotic drum;
- we see ourselves as a tolerant fair-minded people, yet treat refugees in detention in ways completely contrary to these basic cultural values;
- we recognise that Indigenous Australians are amongst the most disadvantaged in our society, yet we continue to show cultural insensitivity in trying to remedy the situation;

- we see ourselves as an independent country with distinctive cultural attributes, yet we have shelved any discussion of how we can better reflect that independence in our constitutional arrangements; and
- we profess the virtues of intercultural dialogue and mutual understanding between nations, yet we abstain from supporting an international cultural convention aimed at achieving these very objectives.

The last-mentioned of these refers to Australia's disgraceful abstention from joining 148 other countries in approving UNESCO's Cultural Diversity Convention in October 2005—an egregious action that was reversed in due course by the incoming Rudd Government.

A look at the issues noted above brings a sobering realisation: apart from some detail, they are still broadly relevant today. Certainly we can say that under the Turnbull Liberal/National Coalition Government we have an administration that has cut funding to the arts, that oversees this country's unconscionable treatment of refugees in detention, that has rejected the reasonable request put by Indigenous Australians for a say in how they are governed, and that shows no interest in reviving discussion about a republic. Perhaps it is a case of *plus ça change*. In the following pages I discuss whether this is so.

1. The context: what is cultural policy today?

Background

Misunderstandings abound around the nature and scope of cultural policy, so before embarking on contemporary Australia, we need to understand the wider context within which the concept of a government's cultural policy has evolved.[4] In the 1970s and 1980s, the major concern of most countries' cultural policies was with the creative arts—how they contribute to a civilised society, how more people could be introduced to the benefits of artistic consumption, and how the arts content of education systems and the media could be improved. For example, a report in 1980 by the first Executive Officer of the Australia Council for the Arts, Jean Battersby, outlined a range of measures that described Australian cultural policy at the time as exclusively related to the arts.[5] Since those early days there has been a transformation in the ways in which cultural policy is interpreted and practised around the world, arising for both cultural and economic reasons. In the cultural arena, the scope of cultural policy has expanded from a concern solely with the arts, to embrace a broader interpretation of culture as a way of life. Parallel with this has been a breakdown of the old equation of 'the arts' with 'high culture'. Although pockets of resistance remain, the pejorative distinction between high and popular culture, or between the high and popular arts, is now largely outdated. Instead, cultural products and consumption practices are more commonly seen to lie along a trajectory whose dimensions are described in terms like commercial/non-commercial, traditional/avant-garde, large-/small-scale, mass/specialised, majority/minority, and so on. So, as the usage of the term 'culture' has continued to extend beyond its high-art interpretation, the range of cultural activities of interest to policy has widened.

While an expansion in the *cultural* concerns for a cultural policy might be welcomed, indicating a more inclusive engagement with the cultural life of the nation, the impact on cultural policy-making of changes in the *economic* environment have been viewed far less favourably. The major economic transformation that has affected the world over the last twenty years has, of course, been globalisation, a process driven by the digital revolution, the explosion in computational power available across a wide range of applications—the growth of the internet and the invention of new devices for communication and data transmission. In addition, the emergence of a global marketplace for many commodities has been enabled by a widespread acceptance of neoliberal economic principles as the basis for national and international policy-making.

The cultural and economic impacts of globalisation have been profound, nowhere more so than in the ways in which the digital world has grown in sophistication and become established as an essential component of the life and work of artists, creative workers, commercial and non-commercial firms producing and distributing cultural product, cultural agencies and institutions, and consumers. In one way or another, these developments have been apparent in the financial environment in which cultural production takes place, in both the commercial and the not-for-profit sectors of the cultural industries. In these circumstances cultural policy on the supply side struggles to keep up, becoming increasingly marginalised as the neoliberal agenda of smaller government and expanded corporate power takes hold. On the demand side, new generations of consumers are using the internet, mobile telephony and digital media in ways that not only expand their range of cultural experience but may actually transform them from passive recipients of cultural messages into active co-creators of cultural content. The sense of empowerment brought about by these developments, and the process of re-defining cultural identities that they initiate, are likely to continue as significant influences on the content of cultural policy.

The creative economy and the cultural industries

The trends described above have had a direct influence on the development of cultural policy in recent years, pushing it towards becoming an arm of economic policy, with an emphasis on the potential of the so-called creative sector to generate employment, exports and economic growth—key objectives in any government's economic agenda.[6] The co-option of cultural policy into this agenda derives from the emerging concept of the 'creative economy', the idea that a creative sector can be identified within the macro-economy as a particular source of economic dynamism in the new information age. The creative economy concept has its origins in the proposition that creativity, whether in art, science, technology or commerce, is a key factor in generating economic success both for individual businesses and for whole economies. Creativity, it is argued, is a prerequisite for innovation, and innovation is the driver of technological change—which in turn boosts productivity and eventually economic growth. The rhetoric of the creative economy has been adopted and developed in countries like the UK, for example, where a group of thirteen creative industries was set up in 1997, and which still figures prominently in British policy-making today.[7] In countries of the global South the creative economy concept has also been pushed as a potential source of cultural and economic development in a series of reports from the UN Conference on Trade and Development, UNESCO, and the UN Development Program.[8]

Application of the creative economy idea to the specifically cultural industries depends on harnessing the power of artistic creativity to economic purposes, beginning with art and proceeding through artistic creativity, creativity in general, innovation, technological progress, competitive advantage, leading in due course to growth in incomes, exports, employment and other indicators of economic success. In many developed countries over the past decade, the cultural industries can indeed be shown to have grown faster than other sectors like manufacturing and agriculture, when measured in terms of value of output or levels of employment.[9] Thus is rhetoric converted into fact, and the economic legitimacy of cultural policy is assured.

Do these trends imply a takeover of cultural policy by narrow-minded culturally-insensitive economists, driven by a solely instrumental view of the policy process? Would such a takeover subordinate the lofty purposes of culture to the sordid demands of the marketplace—a commodification of culture consistent with the gloomy forecasts that Theodor Adorno and Max Horkheimer pronounced seventy years ago?[10] If it is true that neoliberalism has re-defined culture in its own image, a world where the individual replaces the collective and the market is relied upon to deliver all our needs, then there are grounds for pessimism; in these circumstances policy becomes drained of any relevance other than as a servant of the economy. The cultural industries are reduced to being just another economic sector.

However, there is an alternative interpretation of the cultural industries and their economic role, one that reorients their purpose away from the economic and towards their cultural rationale. This alternative approach places the core creative arts at the centre of the cultural sector instead of on the periphery. It assumes that the cultural content of the outputs produced within the sector springs from the incorporation of creative ideas that originate in the arenas of primary artistic practice. This is the so-called concentric circles model, whose distinctive feature is that it conflates this central role into the wider context of the cultural industries more broadly defined, by surrounding the arts with the industries that derive their cultural content from the creative core.[11] The successive circles extend as far as commercial activities such as advertising and fashion, which have relatively small cultural content.

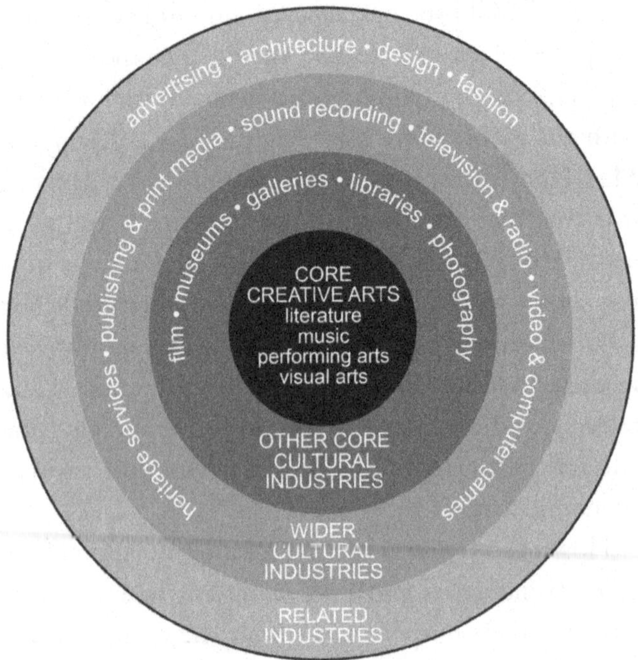

In its basic form the model comprises four circles:

- *Core creative arts*: literature, music, performing arts, visual arts;
- *Other core cultural industries*: film, museums, galleries, libraries, photography;
- *Wider cultural industries*: heritage services, publishing and print media, sound recording, television and radio, video and computer games;
- *Related industries*: advertising, architecture, design, fashion.

The model recognises that the creative ideas generated in the core by artists and arts organisations have a life of their own and exist quite independently of whether or not they might have some economic potential. Their production gives rise to enormous public value in animating discussion, interaction, reflection about our culture, a value that can be conveniently referred to as part of their cultural value in order to distinguish it from any economic value the ideas may generate. By emphasising the cultural value that is created right across the cultural sector, the concentric circles model represents a recalibration of thinking about value in the cultural industries away from an obsessive preoccupation with the financial contribution of art and culture to the economy.

Nevertheless, the model specifically identifies an economic role for the cultural sector; it sees the capacity of the wider cultural industries to generate economic value as being dependent ultimately on the supply of ideas and creative talent originating in the core arts. Thus arts funding, which may be provided for the best cultural reasons relating to the pursuit of purely artistic objectives, can also lead to a possible economic payoff. The way is thus opened to a cultural policy where economic outcomes are admitted as relevant to the policy-making process without becoming a dominating influence on the policy's direction.

Cultural policy in action: the case of the UK

How has the evolving concept of cultural policy at a global level been incorporated into the ways in which cultural policies are being framed? An example serves to illustrate these processes: the case of the United Kingdom.

Current cultural policy in the UK is enshrined in a White Paper released by the then Minister for Culture and the Digital Economy, Ed Vaizey MP, in March 2016.[12] It was the first White Paper for culture published in more than fifty years, the only previous one having been Jennie Lee's much-quoted White Paper for the arts in 1965. The objectives of the UK cultural policy are summarised as:

- to increase participation in the arts and cultural life, through education, training and attention to cultural diversity;

- to enable communities across the country to benefit from 'the riches of our culture', with particular emphasis on heritage;
- to increase Britain's international standing through the further development of the country's soft power;
- to encourage private sector involvement with the cultural sector through a range of investment incentives.

Three aspects of these policy settings are of particular interest to our present discussion. First, although policies for arts support in the UK have traditionally balanced the twin objectives of access and excellence, this cultural policy places a firm emphasis on the former. It appears that the pursuit of artistic excellence is left to the various arts councils to sort out; the cultural policy is interpreted in terms of the inclusive definition of culture aimed at improving access across the whole population. Accordingly the targets are children, through educational programs, and communities via a range of local-level interventions.

Secondly, despite the important role that the creative industries have played in British economic policy over the last twenty years, there is little indication of this in the White Paper. Indeed the development of the cultural industries as a focus for policy engagement is scarcely mentioned, and despite the recent inclusion of 'digital' alongside culture, media and sport in the relevant department's title, the main reference to the new economy is to the digitisation of public collections; aspects such as the possibilities for small business start-ups producing digital cultural product are ignored.[13] Instead the emphasis in the area of cultural investment is on providing greater incentives for private sector involvement in arts and cultural funding.

Finally, there is a strong economic undertone to the policy's interest in advancing British soft power via cultural exports, increased international cultural exchange and cooperation, and promotion of British cultural heritage at home and abroad. So, for example, the GREAT campaign uses culture to promote 'brand Britain',[14] an enterprise that is claimed to have yielded £1.8 billion in 'economic return' to the country over 2012–2015.[15]

Whether the UK cultural policy will deliver on its lofty promises is still a work in progress. While there may be some successes so far, there are also difficulties. There have been complaints about the decline in expenditure on music education; and recent cuts in government support for local libraries—a major locus for citizens' social and cultural engagement—hardly bode well for the policy's ambitious objectives for community cultural development.

2. Cultural policy in Australia since 2006

Since 2006 cultural policy in Australia has experienced something of a roller-coaster ride, as a succession of governments, and an even more rapid succession of prime ministers and ministers for the arts, have introduced and then abandoned a range of measures affecting the arts and the cultural sector. In the following pages I review these events and the various reactions to them, with a view to identifying some important themes of relevance to thinking about the way forward from here. I group the sequence of events into six more or less chronological stages:

- the Australia 2020 Summit (2008),
- *Creative Australia* (2011–2013),
- Review of the Australia Council (2011–2013),
- the National Program for Excellence in the Arts (2015),
- the Catalyst—Arts and Culture Fund (2015–2017),
- the Australia Council (2018 and evermore).

Along the way I make a short digression to consider the shambles that is Australian book industry policy.

The Australia 2020 Summit

The Rudd Labor Government came to power in 2007 on a wave of popular support fuelled by the 'Kevin-07' campaign and the accumulated disillusion amongst the general public with a decade of conservative rule. As Prime Minister, John Howard himself had been the subject of much discontent and lost his own seat of Bennelong in the election. The new Prime Minister moved quickly to make the most of the sense of renewal that a change of government had brought about. One of his first acts, in February 2008, was to deliver a National Apology to the Stolen Generations, directed to the Indigenous children who had been forcibly removed from their families by previous governments and churches. The Apology was an emphatic repudiation of Howard's refusal to take such a step, and its cultural significance has since been widely recognised.

Another activity that Rudd himself initiated early in 2008 was the Australia 2020 Summit. It was an ambitious idea; not since the days of Bob Hawke had there been such a move toward a process of wide-ranging consultation in the formation of public policy. The stated intention of the Summit was to put forward ideas to help stage a long-term strategy for the nation's future, to tackle the fundamental challenges confronting Australia by thinking in new ways.[16] To this end, an extensive program of public consultation was set in train, culminating on 19–20 April 2008 when one thousand invited participants gathered in Parliament House in Canberra for a weekend of discussion. Attendees were allocated into ten groups of 100 each, covering areas such as productivity, the economy, sustainability, health, rural industries, Indigenous affairs, and so on. To some observers the whole show was an exercise in Prime Ministerial self-aggrandisement, but in fact Rudd was deeply engaged at a personal level with the Summit, participating closely throughout and making a closing address which must rank as one of the best speeches of his career.

One of the Summit groups was devoted to the topic Towards a Creative Australia: the Future of the Arts, Film and Design. It was co-chaired by Cate Blanchett, Julianne Schultz and the then Arts Minister, Peter Garrett, and the list of 100 participants making up the group read like a Who's-Who in art and culture of the time. The *leitmotif* for the proceedings was the notion of creativity as a central element in defining the nation, involving its citizens and nurturing its children. The aims of the group identified a need to:

> *implement policies that will produce a sustainable creative sector and support artists, build educational capacity, integrate Indigenous and settler perspectives and recognise the centrality of the arts and creativity to the whole economy. This will result in increased personal capacity and confidence of all citizens, including artists, a stronger economy, and greater international understanding of Australia as a mature, creative, innovative society.*[17]

Discussion focussed particularly on the importance of expanding arts education in schools, the need to develop new investment and support models for the arts, the importance of recognising and protecting Indigenous culture and language, and the desirability of a whole-of-government approach to the arts, culture, design and the creative economy. Some of the recommendations emerging from the Summit were clear and practicable, such as the proposal to introduce 'artists in residence' in schools; others were unspecific and ill-defined, such as the meaningless ambition to 'double cultural output by 2020'. But, despite some occasionally wayward contributions to the debate, the opportunity for such a wide range of participants to indulge in some blue-sky thinking about future directions for Australian cultural life generated a lot of ideas that served as food for thought for policy-makers in the years ahead.

One of the outcomes of the creative stream in the 2020 Summit was a recommendation emphasising the need for a new national cultural and design strategy and policy. This recommendation leads us directly into the next stage in the cultural policy saga.

Creative Australia: the planning, the reality and the aftermath

The first Minister for the Arts in the new Labor Government was Peter Garrett, a rock musician and lead singer in the band Midnight Oil. He appointed a Ministerial Advisory Committee to assist him in the Arts

Portfolio, and a process of considering how to implement the 2020 Summit's proposal for a national cultural strategy was begun. However, Garrett fell victim to the internal division within the Government that culminated in mid-2010 with the removal of Kevin Rudd and the appointment of Julia Gillard as Prime Minister. Garrett was replaced as Arts Minister by Simon Crean who came from a trade union background and was a former Labor Party leader.

These upheavals changed the atmosphere in which the arts were regarded within the Labor Government. Neither Rudd nor Gillard was particularly noted for having strong cultural interests; in fact Rudd had alienated many supporters by his intemperate and uninformed criticism of an exhibition by the respected photographer Bill Henson showing the naked figure of a young girl, even though he had not seen the works himself. Crean came to the Portfolio with a passion for the arts that was to become more and more evident as his involvement in the Portfolio accumulated. He immediately initiated a formal process aimed at developing Australia's first national cultural policy since *Creative Nation*.

The first stage in this process was the preparation of a discussion paper that set out a range of issues, problems and possibilities for a cultural policy.[18] An invitation was issued to the arts and cultural community and to the general public to provide comment and criticism. The paper paid particular attention to ways in which Australia could best position itself in the arts, culture, and creative industries such as film and television, digital technologies and the media. Despite its inevitably aspirational tone, it seemed to promise something more than business-as-usual in cultural policy by offering a range of options indicated for bringing culture into contact with the 'education revolution', with technology and innovation, and with its role in generating social cohesion.[19]

Feedback from the Discussion Paper was duly absorbed by the Departmental staff, the Cultural Policy Reference Group and the Minister, and a full draft of a policy was on track to be released in mid-2012. However, despite Crean's arguments in Cabinet discussions leading to the 2012 Federal Budget, no funding for a cultural policy was in prospect. Accordingly the final production of a complete cultural policy statement was postponed until the following year.

The new cultural policy was finally launched at a National Press Club function in Canberra on 13 March 2013. The policy, entitled *Creative Australia: national cultural policy*, was endorsed by Prime Minister Gillard, and was presented to the Press Club and to the world by Minister Crean. In his speech, Crean spoke of his long-held passion for the arts, and expressed his view of the artist as central to us as a nation and to securing our future. He outlined the aims of the policy to create excellence, jobs, prospects and opportunity, with a particular emphasis on the role of the cultural industries in innovation and employment creation. In short, Crean's vision was one that, in the terms of our discussion earlier, saw a cultural policy generating both cultural value and economic value for the country and its citizens.

The immediate reaction to *Creative Australia* was by and large favourable. Ben Goldsmith, writing in *The Conversation*, described it as 'bold and forward looking', but noted that there would be difficulties ahead.[20] Michael Shmith in the *Sydney Morning Herald* also warned of criticism, but expressed gratitude for a policy with some money attached.[21]

What was the substance of the policy outlined in this 150-page document with its $235 million funding package attached? Its objectives were stated as being to:

- Recognise, respect and celebrate the centrality of Aboriginal and Torres Strait Islander cultures to the uniqueness of Australian identity.
- Ensure that government support reflects the diversity of Australia and that all citizens have a right to shape our cultural identity and its expression.
- Support excellence and the special role of artists as the source of original work and ideas.
- Strengthen the capacity of the cultural sector to contribute to national life, community wellbeing and the economy.
- Ensure Australian creativity thrives in the digitally enabled 21st century, by supporting

innovation, the development of new creative content, knowledge and creative industries.

The policy directions for realising these goals were grouped under three themes:

Theme 1: Modernise funding and support

- Review and structural reform of the Australia Council
- Promotion of a culture of giving, partnership and investment, mentorship and entrepreneurship
- Cooperation, partnership and support between all levels of government

Theme 2: Creative expression and the role of the artist

- Attention to career pathways, cultural leadership skills and expertise
- A universal arts education for lifelong learning
- Innovative content in digital and emerging platforms

Theme 3: Connect to national life for a social and economic dividend

- Recognise the centrality of Indigenous culture in national life
- Foster the creative industries and the creative economy
- Improve access to and management of national collections

- Regional development through community-based arts and culture programs
- Deeper and broader international cultural engagement

Under each theme a number of policy actions were listed, and where relevant, the funding requirements were spelt out. Some of the funding proposals involved new money, others simply listed existing commitments, or the shifting of funding from one area of government to another. A number of the policy actions would presumably be absorbed into existing Departmental workloads.

It is apparent that the content of *Creative Australia* reflects many of the trends in cultural policy development that I discussed earlier. In particular I draw attention to four aspects that stand out. First, the policy incorporates the creative economy into the broad field of cultural policy-making, with all its potential to exploit new technologies and to create employment, without losing sight of the inalienable cultural purpose of this field of government action. Second, the central role of the creative arts and of individual artists in generating both cultural benefits for the people and tangible benefits for the economy, is clearly understood, and is taken on board in the design of policy strategies. Third, inexorable trends in the real world of arts and cultural funding are accepted as dictating needed reforms—to the Australia Council's mode of operation, to the development of new funding models, to the mobilisation of increased private sector engagement and support. And finally, the policy's attention to education is to be welcomed in an era when there is an urgent need for an increased commitment to fostering children's creative involvement in the arts in the public and private school systems.

Simon Crean's cultural policy contains much to praise but not everyone was happy with some aspects.[22] There is not much attention to design, and although film is mentioned, to arrive at a sensible film policy in these uncertain times would take much detailed policy analysis. Likewise, apart from some initiatives to assist the national collecting institutions, there is little mention of tangible cultural heritage, for example in regard to the historic urban environment.

Let us return now to the chronological story. We left it at the point in March 2013 where *Creative Australia* had been released, to the relief of the arts and cultural community that had waited so long. But the joy of those who welcomed the advent of Australia's first cultural policy in two decades was short lived. Less than two weeks later Simon Crean was dismissed, following his ill-judged attempt to overthrow Prime Minister Gillard.[23] His eventual replacement as Arts Minister was Tony Burke, an articulate and committed defender of the arts who promised to pick up *Creative Australia* and run with it with the same determination that his predecessor had shown.[24] However, Party instability continued with the toppling of Julia Gillard in June 2013 and the re-insertion of Kevin Rudd into the prime ministership. Shortly thereafter, on 7 September

2013, a federal election was held at which the Labor Government was defeated and a Coalition government was returned to power, led by Tony Abbott.

Thus *Creative Australia* enjoyed a much shorter life as a formal component of government policy than had *Creative Nation*, which at least existed for long enough for some of its programs to be put into effect. No such action had been possible over the few months in which *Creative Australia* survived. Hopes had been expressed that cultural policy might rise above political allegiances, and the incoming administration might carry the policy forward in a spirit of accord; indeed during discussions in the Reference Group when the policy was being drafted, it had been suggested that it should be so lofty in its intentions, so universal in its appeal, that it would not be jettisoned by a new government but protected by its own virtue—surrounded, as it were, by an Abbott-proof fence. Not surprisingly, such hopes proved unfounded, and the national cultural policy, along with its expenditure proposals, was unceremoniously dumped by the new Federal Government.

Although the national cultural policy of 2013 was never implemented, *Creative Australia* remains a landmark document as the most comprehensive attempt at a national cultural policy statement undertaken by any country in the world in the new millennium. As such it will continue to serve as a reference point in the ongoing debate about the proper role for governments in this field, both in Australia and in the international arena. In this regard the policy may come to enjoy the longevity that has been achieved by *Creative Nation*, which is still referred to in the literature of cultural policy today.[25]

Review of the Australia Council

As a part of the process of developing the national cultural policy, Simon Crean instituted a review of the Australia Council, with the prospect that any agreeable recommendations arising from the review would align with the cultural policy and could in due course be incorporated into an overall strategy for the cultural sector. Two external consultants from corporate backgrounds, Gabrielle Trainor and Angus James, were appointed to undertake the review, which was carried out largely independently from the work of the cultural policy Reference Group. The Review report was published in May 2012 and contained no less than 18 recommendations, the most significant of which sought a more direct ministerial engagement with the affairs of the Council, and proposed a restructuring of the Council's governance.[26] Trainor and James recommended that the Australia Council develop a Strategic Plan to be agreed by the Minister, proposed some new funding for the Council, and suggested a range of measures to improve the flow of private sector support. They recommended abolition of the art-form boards that had been a structural feature of the Council since its inception in the 1970s, and proposed some reforms to the grant assessment procedures.

The Government's response to the review was published as an appendix to the *Creative Australia* document. This somewhat eccentric way of communicating the Government's reaction to the review was apparently intended to make clear the fact that the Australia Council was a part of the process of cultural policy formation, even if a consideration of the Council's role in the arts funding hierarchy had been undertaken independently. In the event, the Government agreed with the majority of the recommendations, although some were agreed to only 'in principle'. An example of the latter was the recommendation that a 'new purpose' be expressed for the Council, supported by four principles which would direct the Council to:

- support work of excellence, at all stages of the artistic lifecycle;
- promote an arts sector that is distinctively Australian;
- ensure that the work it supports has an audience or market; and
- maximise the social and economic contribution made by the arts sector to Australia.

While the first two of these are consistent with the objectives that the Australia Council has pursued ever since its inception, the last two carry implications that are a long way from the concept of an arm's-length arts-supporting organisation. Both of them elevate the economic role of the arts to a level that could potentially overwhelm the artistic or cultural purpose of the creative arts. Even if a liberal view is taken of 'audience' in the third principle, as distinct from the clearly more commercial implication of 'market', the principle still appears to rule out support for the sort of exploratory, innovative, critical, crazy, unclassifiable work whose reception cannot be foreseen and yet whose existence is vital to artistic progress. Likewise the proposal to 'maximise' the social and economic contribution of the arts sector to Australian life sounds a similar alarm. Multiple objectives can't all be maximised simultaneously, so it is likely that maximising the yield of economic value from the arts sector could only be achieved at some cost to the generation of cultural value. The Government's deliberately equivocal response to this recommendation left the door open for a more appropriate reassertion of the Council's role to be formulated in due course.

In a speech on the occasion of the launch of the National Cultural Policy, the Australia Council chair, Rupert Myer, commented on the Review's recommendations and the Government's response to them.[27] He welcomed the provision of an additional $73.3 million over four years to assist the Council in its core responsibility to support more artists who have achieved excellence in practice, and committed the Council to cooperate in modernising the legislation under which it operates in order to clarify functions and remove constraints.

There was sufficient time between publication of the

Trainor/James Review in May 2012 and the demise of the Labor Government in September 2013 for those recommendations found acceptable by the Government to be acted upon. Accordingly a new Act was drafted and passed in June 2013, despite some disquiet that had been expressed about it within the arts community.[28] By the time the Government changed, the Review's proposals for restructuring the Australia Council were a *fait accompli*, the old art-form boards had been disbanded, and a new Council had been appointed. Since then the Australia Council has been back in the news and the arts policy caravan has rolled on, as we shall see further below.

The reign of George Brandis as Arts Minister 2013–15

The accession of the Coalition Government on 14 September 2013 saw Tony Abbott take over as Prime Minister and Senator George Brandis appointed as Minister for the Arts, a portfolio he held alongside his major role as Attorney-General. Brandis was known to have personal interests in, and firm opinions about, the arts—he believed strongly in 'excellence' which he associated primarily with the work of the major performing companies in theatre, opera and ballet.[29] He also had well-established literary interests, and indeed was known in some quarters as 'Bookshelves Brandis' on account of his insistence on accommodating a large collection of books in his Parliament House office.

He saw an important role for government to nurture 'high quality' art in its provision of funding to support the sector, and was not convinced that this was being achieved under current funding arrangements.

A foretaste of things to come appeared in March 2014, barely six months into his term as Arts Minister. A group of artists boycotted the 19th Sydney Biennale in protest at sponsorship of the event by Transfield Holdings, a private company investing in major infrastructure, associated in this instance with the operation of detention centres for refugees being held in Nauru and on Manus Island.[30] It could be suggested that the artists' protest might have had more relevance if it had been directed at the Government which was implementing this cruel and detestable policy, rather than at the contractor that was simply doing the Government's bidding. Moreover, collateral damage arising from the artists' actions included the resignation from the Biennale board of its Chair, Luca Belgiorno-Nettis, a member of the family that had for 40 years been major philanthropic supporters of the arts and continues to play that role today. Be that as it may, protecting the right of artists to express provocative and unpopular views has always been essential in enabling the arts to fulfil their role in informing progressive social policy.

But all this was too much for Brandis. On 12 March 2014 he wrote to the Australia Council, instructing it to develop a policy to govern the funding of clients who chose to reject corporate support. The Council is an independent statutory body perfectly capable of making funding decisions according to its terms of reference, and indeed had already declined to be associated with a range of companies in industries such as tobacco and gambling. In responding to this request, the Council would have been justified in telling the Minister to get lost. In the event, realpolitik dictated a more sober reply: the Council assured the Minister that it would take his advice on board in the formulation of its forthcoming Strategic Plan.

Nevertheless, over the coming months Brandis' intervention in the Sydney Biennale case presaged a more hands-on role for the Arts Minister in the formulation of cultural policy. And so indeed it came to pass. The first signs of this appeared in the Abbott Government's first Budget, delivered by Treasurer Joe Hockey in May 2014. This budget was judged at the time and subsequently to be both economically and politically inept; and as far as the arts sector was concerned, the news was not encouraging. Amounts allocated to the arts in the year 2014–15 together with the forward estimates revealed a cut of about $100 million over four years. The Australia Council's share of the cuts ($28 million) included a directive that effectively quarantined funding for the 28 major performing arts companies, which included all the Minister's favourites. The biggest single cut ($38 million) was borne by Screen Australia. The biggest losers, however, proved to be small-to-medium enterprises across the arts, and individual artists—in other words those most engaged with new, cutting-edge and innovative work.[31]

But these 2014 assaults on the level and direction of arts funding under Brandis were as nothing compared to his intervention in May 2015. Observers both inside and outside the arts sector were astonished to learn on Budget Night that about $110 million in Australia Council funding over four years would be re-directed to Brandis' own Ministry for the Arts. The re-direction would involve:

- the establishment of a National Program for Excellence in the Arts (NPEA), with funding of $104.7 million over four years;
- transfer of the Visions of Australia program (for touring exhibitions etc.) and support for festivals to the Ministry;
- doubling the Ministry's funding to $1.7 million per year; and
- funding Creative Partnerships Australia for a further three years at a cost of $5.3 million.

The objectives of the NPEA can be summarised as follows:

- to deliver quality arts experiences that grow audiences;
- to strengthen Australia's reputation as a sophisticated and artistic nation internationally;
- to encourage greater private sector funding; and

- to support initiatives in specific regions or priority areas.

The new Program's title indicated that 'quality' in the first of these objectives meant 'excellence'; it was this characteristic that would underpin the achievement of the other objectives in the list. It was not spelt out how an agreed interpretation of excellence might be arrived at. The second and third objectives simply took over functions already provided for in the Australia Council's remit, while the last one laid out, unmistakeably, the potential for some judicious pork-barrelling in advance of future elections.

In announcing these policy changes, the Minister affirmed his earlier decision that funding for the major performing arts companies would not be affected. This assurance reflected the Minister's personal tastes referred to above; in fact in June 2014 he declared that:

> *I'm more interested in funding arts companies that cater to the great audiences that want to see quality drama, music or dance, than I am in subsidising individual artists responsible only to themselves.*[32]

Not surprisingly such an unprecedented shift in arts funding policy generated a great deal of criticism and indeed outrage.[33] In regard to the Australia Council, the transfers combined with the required savings via the efficiency dividend represented an annual reduction in its funding of about 13 per cent over four years, with impacts that would, as noted earlier, fall most heavily on individual artists and the small-to-medium sector.

But the strongest criticisms were directed at the terms of reference for the new funding program to be delivered by the NPEA, whose establishment represented the most extensive assertion of ministerial power over the direction of arts policy that had been experienced in Australia in the past half century. There are a number of jurisdictions both internationally and at the Australian State/Territory level where a minister has direct responsibility for the ultimate approval of arts grants, but it is difficult to think of a case where the shaping of criteria is so reflective of the personal predilections of the minister in charge, or where the likely pattern of grants would be so different from that which would have emerged under traditional arms-length funding arrangements.

Brandis remained impervious to the mounting criticism of his actions. However, as it turned out, political upheavals once again intervened, this time affecting the conservative side of politics. On 14 September 2015 Tony Abbott was replaced as Prime Minister by Malcolm Turnbull, and in the ministerial realignment that followed, Brandis' tenure of the Arts Portfolio was terminated.

Before continuing with the chronological story, I want to step aside for a moment to refer to a particular area that provides a case-study illustrating much of what has characterised the process of cultural policy formulation in Australia under both Labor and Coalition governments over the past ten years—the field of books, literature and the publishing industry.

Book industry policy 2009 to the present[34]

The book industry in Australia is contained within one of the middle circles in the concentric circles model of the cultural sector. It has a strong commercial orientation in the production and marketing of a wide range of trade and educational books, and also makes a significant contribution to Australian cultural life, via its role in publishing literary fiction and other creative work. The presence of these two contrasting dimensions to the value that this industry generates presents a dilemma for the policy-maker: should the book industry be regarded as an industrial or a cultural sector? If the former, a government's dealing with the industry will be motivated by economic concerns and any assistance deemed necessary on these grounds will form part of overall economic policy. If on the other hand the production of books is regarded as a cultural industry, policy towards the industry will fall into the ambit of the government's cultural policy, and the motive for supporting it, if support is warranted, will be to pursue primarily cultural, not necessarily economic, objectives. This dilemma has troubled Australian governments for many years, and has had a significant effect on the direction of book industry policy.

In view of the stresses on the industry being imposed by digital disruption that were growing more intense, the Labor Government in April 2010 initiated a review of the book industry. The review was established as the Book Industry Strategy Group (BISG) by the then Minister for Innovation, Industry, Science and Research, Senator Kim Carr, whose interest in the book industry was well known. It was chaired by former politician and celebrated polymath Barry Jones. The fact that the BISG was operating under an industry rather than an Arts or Cultural ministry meant that its deliberations had to be orientated towards economic rather than cultural concerns, and its recommendations had to address issues of economic rather than cultural policy. Accordingly its recommendations had a strong economic flavour; they included: integrating the book supply chain; competing in the global market; improving efficiencies; rewarding and protecting creativity; supporting the business environment; and supporting Australian culture.[35]

One of the BISG's recommendations was that a Book Industry Collaborative Council (BICC) be established to carry forward the implementation of the BISG's reform priorities. Thus does one government process give rise to another. The new Council, set up under the auspices of a new Industry Minister, Greg Combet, began operation on 1 July 2012, with a 12-month timeframe to complete its work. The 20-member Council comprised representatives from peak book industry associations and experts in fields related to the book industry. It was chaired by the present author. As with the BISG, the BICC's operations were set up within the Industry Portfolio, and hence its terms of reference and its ultimate recommendations were firmly focussed on industry-led reform. Nevertheless, the Council recognised that the book industry's claim on the attention of government lay primarily in its cultural role, and pointed out that book industries in many countries 'have become a focus for public policy because [...] they provide a link between the production of economic benefits and the generation of cultural value'.[36] Thus the Council devoted a section of its report to discussing the ways in which books contribute to the literary and broader culture and to pointing out that the cultural importance of the Australian book industry is manifest at all points in the supply chain from author to reader.[37]

The final BICC Report was presented to the Government on 28 June 2013. However, it too was caught up in the political turmoil of the time in which Kevin Rudd was returned as Prime Minister. Senator Carr moved back into the industry portfolio, but there was no time for a response to the BICC Report—only a few weeks later the Labor Government was removed from office. Thus the Report, which contained the most comprehensive blueprint for reform that had ever been put together for the Australian book industry, suffered the same fate as *Creative Australia*, a victim to the power struggles that characterise Australian political life and undermine any effort at rational long-term policy-making.

The game was not entirely lost, however. One of the BICC's recommendations was that a new Australian Book Council be set up to oversee the implementation of the BICC's recommendations, financed by the industry but with some government seeding money. It was unlikely that the new Industry Department would welcome this proposal, but among some former members of the BICC it was thought that now Brandis was Arts Minister, he might warm to the idea if it were presented as a matter for cultural rather than industry policy, given his devotion to books that we have noted.

Indeed these speculations proved well-founded. In October 2014 at a meeting with some former BICC members, Senator Brandis confirmed that the book industry was much more likely to receive a sympathetic hearing from him than from the Industry Portfolio, and in due course policy responsibility for the Australian book industry effectively moved to the Arts Portfolio. Thus the focus of book policy was transferred from economic policy to cultural policy.

As had been expected, the idea of a Book Council was the one that appealed to Brandis, and discussions about it proceeded in the Minister's office and in consultation with Prime Minister Abbott. This process culminated on 8 December 2014 at the Prime Minister's Literary Awards ceremony held at a dinner in the National Gallery of Victoria. In his speech to the assembled book industry players, the Prime Minister announced that his Government would set up a Book Council of Australia with funding of $2 million per year over three years. However, the industry's joy at this announcement was considerably soured when it learned on the same evening that this funding would not be new money, but deducted from the budget of the Australia Council.[38]

The Minister for the Arts ignored continuing criticism surrounding these funding arrangements and in the first months of 2015 proceeded with planning for his new Book Council. A chair and members were appointed, objectives were laid out, and governance and operational issues for the new body were decided. However, before it could hold its first meeting, Malcolm Turnbull was Prime Minister and Brandis had lost the Arts Ministry. The Book Council was put on hold until the 2015 Prime Minister's Literary Awards night on 14 December. It was now Turnbull's turn to make a speech about the book industry. In it the Prime Minister succeeded in alienating the entire industry, first by declaring that he supported the Productivity Commission's latest recommendation to scrap the long-standing Parallel Import Restrictions for books, and then by announcing that the Book Council would be abolished.[39] He offered the gratuitous observation that authors would go on producing books regardless of these decisions. Hopes for the emergence of a rational book policy to sustain the industry into the future had proved to be short-lived.

I have introduced this brief excursion into a specific field of cultural policy because it illustrates the problems and possibilities for cultural policy-making in the contemporary Australian environment. In the first place it demonstrates how rational policy for a cultural sector cannot be invented on the run but demands a deliberative process. The Reports of both the BISG and the BICC represent exemplary cases of this, whereby the voices of all stakeholders were brought together and generated sound policy proposals. Yet even when such processes are followed, their good work can be overturned in an instant by changing political fortunes.

Secondly, experience surrounding the rise and fall of the Book Council exposed the fragility of ad hoc decision-making. The proposal for a Council was never subject to any feasibility assessment, no detailed budget was put forward, and the funding amount for it was arbitrarily determined and obtained by underhand means. The subsequent decision to kill it off was just as arbitrary. Such erratic behaviour at the highest levels of policy-making has occurred all too frequently in recent times, and not only in relation to the arts and cultural sector.

Minister Fifield and life after Brandis

Let us return now to the narrative of the evolution of Australian cultural policy which we left at the point in October 2015 where Malcolm Turnbull acceded to the Prime Ministership in place of Tony Abbott. Given the upheavals in the arts that had played out over the previous year, it was clear that George Brandis would no longer be welcome as Arts Minister. Accordingly he was replaced by Senator Mitch Fifield, who may not have been particularly knowledgeable about the arts but who declared himself a keen supporter. He also held the Communications Portfolio, an area that was likely to absorb the great majority of his attention. Fifield's initial task was to repair the damage that had been wrought by his predecessor's actions. He moved immediately to dismantle the NPEA and replace it with a new program to be called Catalyst—Australian Arts and Culture Fund, launched on 20 November 2015 with an initial funding allocation of $12 million per year. Some of the money released from the NPEA was returned to the Australia Council ($32 million over four years).

Catalyst was designed to fund innovative projects from arts and cultural organisations that would not generally have been eligible for funding from other Australian Government sources. Although it would accept projects from galleries, libraries, archives and museums, there was an expectation that the small-to-medium sector of the arts would become a particular focus, in order to rectify to some extent the harm to this sector that had been caused by previous funding decisions. Catalyst also aimed to support increased access and participation in regional areas, as well as forging new creative and financial partnerships in line with the Government's desire to diversify arts funding sources.

Although there was widespread relief at the demise of the NPEA, Catalyst was not without its critics. Apart from replacing 'excellence' with 'innovation' as an objective, and including a mention of small-to-medium organisations, its terms of reference were not all that different from those of the program it replaced.

Moreover some of its initial grants went to some of the major performing arts companies that had been quarantined from the earlier cuts to Australia Council funding, and there was an element of pork-barrelling in some of its grants.[40]

The May 2016 Budget came and went, the Turnbull Government was re-elected with a much reduced majority, the Catalyst program continued, and little happened to change the unsatisfactory state of Australian cultural policy through the rest of that year.[41] Then in the Federal Budget handed down on 9 May 2017, Catalyst was quietly killed off and it was announced that the majority of funds allocated to Catalyst would be returned to the Australia Council on 1 July. It was noted that project funding commitments already approved would be honoured, and that the Department for the Arts would retain $2 million per year. In total it was expected that an amount of around $80 million would be restored to the Australia Council over four years, comprising the Catalyst money and previously returned funds. Nevertheless the Council's overall allocation was still less than it had received from the previous Labor Government.[42]

During its two-and-a-half years' existence, the Catalyst fund disbursed a total of $35.4 million to 189 projects, funding just over 20 per cent of the applications it received. The money was distributed more or less proportionately across States and Territories, and about fifty-fifty between metropolitan and regional areas. The majority of the funding (84 per cent of projects supported) went to small-to-medium organisations.

What can we say in writing Catalyst's obituary? It was born as a compromise between maintaining an indefensible program for the funding of excellence, and reversing policy entirely by returning to the original status quo. Catalyst was seen as a means for the Government to re-invent its arts funding arrangements by responding to well-articulated criticism in a manner that did not look like a total U-turn. But the new structure occupied a somewhat awkward place in the Federal Government's cultural funding arrangements. Its objectives of promoting access, innovation, participation, international representation, financial partnerships and so on were already well served via existing channels of support, so the need for a new agency with its attendant administrative requirements was not apparent. Moreover, its assessment processes differed significantly from the usual arm's-length and peer review procedures that have traditionally characterised arts funding decision-making in Australia. Thus it could not avoid being accused of serving special interests or being influenced by political expediencies in its determination of which projects to support.

The Australia Council: present and future

Over the entire period covered by this review, the Australia Council has occupied a central and always contested space in the implementation of Australian cultural policy, despite the fact that its annual allocation has comprised less than ten per cent of total cultural funding by the Federal Government, and an even smaller percentage (less than five per cent) when cultural funding is aggregated across all tiers of government.[43] It has remained the focal point for discussion about the delivery of public support for the arts. It was founded in 1975 on the twin principles of arm's length from government in its statutory structure, and the adoption of peer-review processes in its decision-making. Both of these principles have remained steadfastly in place throughout the Council's history, endorsed by governments of all political persuasions and reiterated every time a review of the Council's operations has been undertaken.

Nevertheless, despite the resilience of these foundational principles, the way the Council operates has been subject to a range of criticisms over the years. Three particular strands to the debate can be identified. First, the pursuit of excellence, as provided for in the Council's charter, is argued to be a chimera. Ben Eltham, a leading critic of the concept as a criterion for arts funding, has argued that excellence has become a code word equated to a 'high art' view of culture.[44] He sees ample evidence for this in the co-option of this term in the Brandis policy of unashamed support for the major performing companies presenting what Eltham has previously referred to as the 'heritage' arts (a most inappropriate term), the canonical works in Western music, opera, dance and drama.[45]

To evaluate this criticism, it is necessary to look

more closely at how questions of quality are judged. Of course there is no universal standard, and one person's excellent art may be another person's rubbish. But the Australia Council has to make decisions between alternative funding proposals, and one criterion must revolve around quality. No theatre company wants to put on poor quality work, and no funding body wants to support low quality proposals; in both cases the 'quality' being considered is a multi-faceted concept relating to all aspects of the work under consideration. Eltham's interpretation of the concept of excellence in the Brandis narrative is undoubtedly correct, but this is a restrictive interpretation. A wider view of approaches to quality judgements in the arts is necessary if we are to make funding decisions, and such a wider view is implied in the way in which the Australia Council is set up to make its grant determinations.

The second and related strand to the debate about the Australia Council relates to the claim that the grant-making process has been captured by a small in-group of self-serving artists who use the system to distribute funds to their mates. Whilst this description may overstate the point, it can at least be said that the peer review system may tend to favour grant applicants who are established and recognised at the expense of those who are unknown and difficult to classify. A more wide-ranging criticism of peer review is that artists may not always be the most experienced or best informed amongst potential judges, a criticism similar to that occasionally directed at the jury system to the effect that those charged with making life-or-death decisions about their peers may not be properly equipped to do so.

With some prompting from the political arena and elsewhere, the Australia Council has tried to broaden its decision-making capability whilst retaining the core role of artists in the process. The introduction of 'consumer representatives' into the tent, however, must be viewed with some concern; if consumer preferences had been allowed to determine the fate of Stravinsky's 'Rite of Spring', for example, the work would not have been heard again after its first performance. The question ultimately is whether or not peer review delivers the best-informed decisions, free of cronyism. And the answer would seem to be: not necessarily. It is worth noting that Arts Council England (one of the successors to the former Arts Council of Great Britain) abandoned peer review many years ago in favour of a system that still involves peer assessments at an earlier stage, but that relies on a more focussed input of art-form expertise to sort out final decisions. It appears that the introduction of changed procedures allowed significant cost savings, streamlined the processing of grant applications, and did not generate a negative reaction from the field. There are grounds for carrying out a feasibility study to test reaction to the possible introduction of such a system here.

Finally, the Australia Council has been seen as standing in the way of a more progressive arts policy, since its formal structure leads to inertia and lack of adaptability. This criticism implies that the Council cannot stay abreast of, let alone ahead of, new directions in a dynamic and ever-changing arts environment. To the extent that this criticism is aimed at the Council's support for companies presenting the so-called heritage arts, it is misdirected, partly because the Council's hands are tied by an overarching requirement handed down by the Government, but more importantly because presentation of the heritage arts can indeed be dynamic, forward-looking, artistically adventurous, and entirely relevant to contemporary culture. At the same time it is true that any arts funding body has to run hard to keep up with technological developments that are transforming both the production and consumption of art in the modern world, and inevitably it is likely to fall behind.

Underlying all of these criticisms lurks a persistent problem that affects the way funding decisions can be interpreted. As an economist, I would refer to this as a productivity question—what is the marginal effect of an extra dollar of funding when allocated to a given recipient? To put it more vividly, taking $1,000 off the amount given to Opera Australia, say, in a given year would have a negligible effect on the company's output, whereas transferring the same amount to a small theatre company would be likely to have a significant impact on its work; in other words the productivity of the marginal dollar differs greatly between its uses. It must be said at once that equalising marginal benefits across allocations, as a simple-minded economist might advocate, is certainly not an appropriate decision rule when issues of fixed costs and a multiplicity of funding objectives apply. Nevertheless, given that most public expenditure decisions are made incrementally or decrementally, it would be interesting to look at the marginal impacts of funding re-alignments that have been undertaken by the Council in the past to shed light on these productivity questions, and as a possible guide for future decision-making.

I noted earlier that during the ascendancy of George Brandis as Arts Minister, the Australia Council undertook to prepare a Strategic Plan. It did so, and released it in October 2014, to cover the five-year period to 2019. Entitled *A Culturally Ambitious Nation*, the plan is built around four 'goals', even if the articulation of the goals is in the form of statements rather than as a set of objectives. They are described as follows:

- Australian arts are without borders;
- Australia is known for its great art and artists;
- the arts enrich daily life for all;
- Australians cherish Aboriginal and Torres Strait Islander arts and culture.

The plan is put forward with the usual declarations as to the importance of the arts in all aspects of Australian life and articulates in general terms the ways in which the Council will act to fulfil its ambitious intentions. In particular the Plan directly addresses the criticisms noted above by asserting that 'we will continue to fund excellent art across all art forms [...] we will adapt the way we invest in the arts to [...] become more open and reflective of evolving arts practice'. In the latter respect, the Council says it will 'foster experimentation and risk-taking in all art forms [...] and will continue to invest in initiatives that drive innovation and artistic vibrancy in arts organisations'.

Criticism of the Australia Council and debate about its operations will continue, but it is absurd to suggest its abolition. If we are going to continue providing public support for the arts, and no one is arguing otherwise, we need a mechanism for distributing it. There appears to be no enthusiasm for handing all decision-making responsibility back to Ministers or bureaucrats, so there is little alternative but to continue as we are. The Australia Council Act has recently been updated, the Strategic Plan has been released, the Council's internal structures have been reviewed. It has had to cope with turbulent times in its funding situation, and it continues to remain seriously underfunded, a constraint on how well it can deliver on its wide range of objectives. We should give it time now to show that it can respond to criticism, and regain the confidence and trust of the community.[46]

3. Current issues for a revisited cultural policy

There are many lessons to be drawn from the sad meandering tale that represents the progress, if it can be called that, of Australian cultural policy over the last ten years that we have charted in these pages. Some of these lessons are encouraging—for example, as Australians we have shown that we can indeed countenance a coherent national cultural policy if the mood so takes us. Some of the lessons are profoundly discouraging, such as the sense that good policy is fragile, it can be replaced by bad policy, and in the end does anyone really care? I want to pull together some of these lessons into an assessment of where we can go from here, but before doing so I shall discuss in this section some of the important issues and areas for concern that are of continuing relevance to any discussion of cultural policy in Australia today. The list of issues that I draw attention to below is selective rather than comprehensive, and is presented in no particular order of priority.

Indigenous art and culture

Whatever else is included under the umbrella of an Australian cultural policy, the art and culture of Aboriginal and Torres Strait Islander people will be there. This component of our culture permeated both *Creative Nation* and *Creative Australia*; in both documents the importance of the long tradition of Indigenous culture in allowing all Australians to share in a sense of a common cultural identity is repeatedly stressed. A celebration of Aboriginal art and culture serves as an entry point for many Australians in understanding what Indigenous culture means and how it is practised. For example, the Australia Council's Strategic Plan points to its initiatives in audience development and market promotion as avenues towards increased exposure of Indigenous theatre, dance, music, writing, film and visual art to the rest of the country.

But there is another aspect of Aboriginal and Torres Strait Islander affairs that has significant implications for cultural policy—the importance of culture in dealing with Indigenous disadvantage. The hard-line approach derived from Western models of development argues that the only way forward in improving the circumstances of Aboriginal people is by requiring them to join the modern economy. But interventions aimed at improving the economic and social status of Indigenous Australians are bound to fail when they impose Western cultural norms on people whose culture derives from a very different tradition. Some Ministers responsible for Indigenous Affairs have understood this, but by and large they have been unable to counter a relentless pressure from those who believe that promoting economic development regardless of cultural considerations is the only solution.

One issue that has come to particular prominence in this respect has been the sustainability of communities in remote and very remote regions of Australia. The withdrawal of support for some communities in Western Australia judged to be 'unsustainable', and Tony Abbott's infamous remark about 'lifestyle choice', have focussed attention on the question of the long-term prospects for Indigenous people in remote areas. It is too often not recognised that the cultural capital of Aboriginal and Torres Strait Islander people—the proud inheritance of millennia—represents a cultural asset that can be drawn upon to yield both economic and social development in remote communities, with consequent benefits in strengthening the communities' sustainability. The production of artistic goods and services in remote areas can be a source of economic empowerment for Indigenous Australians. It is by no means a universal panacea, but it does at least offer the prospect of contributing to economic development in ways that enhance rather than override local cultural values.[47]

Fortunately there are some policy initiatives both at Federal and at State/Territory levels that recognise the importance of art and cultural activity for the economic, social and cultural lives of Indigenous people. Of particular importance in this respect are the well-established art centres that are dotted across the length and breadth of remote Australia.[48] These remarkable organisations are an invaluable community resource for the promotion of art practice, cultural engagement, and social cohesion. They provide facilities for Indigenous artists to work and channels for marketing what they produce. Some have been able to move beyond the visual arts to include film, television, music, etc. in their coverage. Government funding has been essential in setting up the art centres and keeping them going, but there is never enough. Reviews of the art centre movement have pointed to the need for further financial support to enable the centres to continue their vital work.[49]

In addition there are other areas of government action that do comprehend the cultural landscape in policy delivery for Aboriginal people: support for the preservation and documentation of Indigenous languages, for example, and the promotion of bilingual education in schools. There is also policy interest in supporting Indigenous enterprises in areas such as cultural tourism, where cultural advancement and employment creation can go hand in hand. In the Aboriginal arts more directly, there exists a number of support programs for performing companies and individual artists working across the whole spectrum of the arts, with distinctive voices that address a range of artistic, cultural, social, political and environmental issues.

Despite these positive indications, however, there remains a black cloud hanging over any effort towards a proper treatment of Indigenous people within Australian cultural policy. As is well known, the Uluru Statement from the Heart, 2017, put forward in good faith after an extensive consultation process,[50] was summarily rejected by the Federal Government. The proposal for a voice in how Aboriginal people are governed was wilfully misrepresented as being a 'third chamber' in the Parliament, and it was killed off on the baseless assertion that the constitutional change being put forward would have 'zero chance' of being accepted. The prospect of a treaty now seems further away than ever.[51]

The role of the individual artist

Whenever a new survey of practising professional artists in Australia is released, a widespread concern is expressed over the relatively low incomes that artists earn.[52] How can it be that these people who contribute so much to our cultural life are so poorly rewarded? Of course it is true that artists generally do not pursue their chosen career in order to make money, but the fact remains that the arts labour market does not price in a component for the public-good benefits that the work of artists provides.

A starvation wage is a reality not only for the struggling artist trying to get started as an actor, visual artist, or musician. It can also be experienced by established mid-career artists who have spent their lives earning a reputation but not a sufficient income to sustain their work in later life. This problem was exemplified recently by Frank Moorhouse in a sombre essay in which he vividly described the plight of the literary author.[53]

Moorhouse is a writer whose works, published over the last fifty years, have earned him an international following and have generated unequivocal recognition of his significant contribution to Australian letters. He recommends establishment of long-term fellowships for well-established writers to enable them to continue producing without having to worry about their financial circumstances.

There is a wider question involved here, which brings us back to our earlier discussion about the creative economy. Artists are the creative labour force in the cultural industries. From this perspective they may be seen as industrial workers—low paid, unrepresented, condemned to rely on a series of short-term contracts, forced by the working structure of the creative industries to lead precarious economic lives, obliged to bear the risks offloaded on them by their corporate paymasters.[54] Alternatively they can be seen as self-starting entrepreneurs at the forefront of the new economy, developing new technologies, leading in digital innovation, finding ways to apply their creative skills not just to the production of art but in a range of other areas as well.

As it happens, both of these realities are valid. But in our consideration of cultural policy we come round full circle. Whether individual artists are the workforce that keeps our theatres, our galleries or our bookshops continuing to turn out great art, or the tech-savvy creative entrepreneurs in the front lines of the digital revolution, they are at the centre of the concentric circles. They are the source of the talent and the creativity that makes art happen and that keeps the cultural sector alive and growing.

It is abundantly clear that the situation of the individual artist in Australia today must remain a central concern for cultural policy, relevant across all artistic occupations. Over the years the Australia Council has responded to this concern by trying to update its support for artists, but the amounts allocated remain pitifully small in comparison with the funding going to the big performing companies, of which only a relatively minor proportion ends up in the hands of artists. Some other funding agencies don't support individual artists at all. There is an urgent need to look for new ways to ensure the economic survival of the individual practitioner. This is not just a matter for public funding agencies at all levels of government to consider; it also involves corporate and other private sector philanthropy.

International engagement

Cultural diplomacy and the exercise of soft power has been an important element that falls within the ambit of a comprehensive cultural policy. There are both cultural and economic dimensions to the promotion of a country's culture abroad. Here in Australia we have always engaged in cultural exchange with other countries, including through programs such as Asialink Arts, and the cultural engagements pursued by the Department of Foreign Affairs and Trade. In this latter context, the conjunction of foreign affairs and trade is appropriate when the arts are involved, in view of the old adage 'where culture leads, trade follows'.[55] Although such a slogan may seem far-fetched, the fact remains that countries in our region are our major trading partners and economic relations with them are likely to be enhanced if we have a stronger cultural dialogue with them. Thus, although international relationships in the arts have their own artistic rationale, there are also economic reasons for paying more attention to this area.

It is true that we already engage in significant levels of artistic exchange with countries like Japan, China, India and others, propelled both by government and private sector initiatives that may have some economic motivation. But it would be possible to strengthen these endeavours, as part of a more active engagement with international affairs in our cultural policy. For example, we could make it a requirement that a cultural exchange program should precede or accompany every trade mission to one of our regional neighbours.

We might even contemplate some bolder initiatives in this field. For example, consider our diplomatic and trade relationships with North Korea. We have incurred the wrath of this unpredictable and dangerous regime by being seen as a handmaiden of the United States. To counter this impression, we could open a direct dialogue with the North Korean leadership by framing it in cultural rather than strategic terms. We could initiate such a dialogue by sending one of our leading music or dance ensembles to Pyongyang—the Bangarra Dance Company would be an obvious choice, or one of our world-class classical music ensembles such as the Australian Chamber Orchestra, the Brandenburg Orchestra, any of the State orchestras, or the Australian Ballet. A tour to North Korea by any of these groups could open the way to a more cordial relationship between our countries than the usual militaristic posturing. In fact we would only be following an example set by the US when in 2008 it sent the New York Philharmonic to North Korea,[56] a visit that created a far more positive response than would have been experienced had they sent a battleship or a nuclear missile.

Cultural heritage

A neglected area in Australian cultural policy is that relating to cultural heritage, both tangible and intangible. We have been a signatory to the World Heritage Convention since 1974, although most of our inscriptions (12 out of 19) are natural heritage items. We have not accepted or ratified the 2003 Convention for the Safeguarding of Intangible Cultural Heritage, presumably because, unlike the other 177 countries which are signatories, we don't think we have any cultural traditions, practices or skills worth preserving. *Creative Australia* had little to say about any sort of heritage, and the regulatory framework within which heritage is protected and conserved at all tiers of government at the present time is haphazard, uncoordinated and weak, despite the best efforts of the Australian Heritage Council, its various State/Territory counterparts, and voluntary organisations such as the national trusts.

In regard to built heritage, historic buildings owned by corporations or private individuals are often looked after with care and concern, but in too many cases 'redevelopment' means blatant disregard for the public interest. Federal and State governments are themselves important owners of heritage buildings, and they are also responsible for administering the various registers of significant heritage items that are intended to provide some protection and oversight of the nation's stock of important historic buildings. But the resources devoted to monitoring compliance are never enough, opportunities for circumventing regulations appear to be too readily available, and the advice of heritage professionals is too frequently ignored.

One of the problems besetting the administration of heritage policy in Australia is a lack of coordination between jurisdictions, such that there is often inconsistency or confusion regarding obligations and requirements relating to heritage protection at different levels. The Productivity Commission conducted an enquiry into heritage in 2005-06,[57] and although its recommendation that the listing process should be voluntary was widely criticised and never adopted, it did point to needed reforms in public-sector regulatory arrangements in this field.

A further problem is lack of money, so it would make sense to start looking for an alternative funding stream. Fortunately we don't have far to look. In a spirit of unashamed plagiarism, we could copy the British example and set up a Heritage Lottery Fund. In fact such a mechanism would not be new to this country—the building of the Sydney Opera House (now listed as a World Heritage site) was financed by significant funding from the Opera House lotteries. Although in the UK money from the Heritage Lottery Fund was for a time diverted to help finance the London Olympics, this source has been called upon to support an enormous range of approved projects over the 24 years since it was begun. We could do the same here.

Monitoring and evaluation

Progress in implementing any policy needs to be tracked over time, and this requires data. In the cultural arena, the axing by the Federal Government of the National Centre for Culture and Recreation Statistics (NCCRS) of the Australian Bureau of Statistics (ABS) in 2014 dealt a blow to the steady supply of data about arts and culture from the Centre that had contributed so strongly to supporting policy-making in the field. The production of a set of cultural satellite accounts by the ABS in 2013–14 was a commendable project, and the ongoing work of the Statistics Working Group of the former Cultural Ministers Council[58] keeps some sources of data alive. But the time is overdue for reinstating the NCCRS, a move that would greatly assist the making of cultural policy in this country.

The other major source of data about the arts is the Australia Council. It is highly commendable that the

Council has maintained and expanded its research and data generation capacity—a source of information about the arts that goes back to its foundation and has served the arts and wider community well throughout its history.

Conclusions: where to from here?

To conclude, let me return to the question posed in my 2006 paper: Does Australia need a cultural policy? We went through the business of formulating one in 2011-2013, but since then much has changed in the arts and in the cultural arena more generally. In the former area, developments include: there has been a succession of changes in the Federal Government's rationale for providing public support for the arts; the means for delivering arts funding have been restructured; the circumstances of individual artists have fluctuated but have shown little improvement; the small-to-medium sector in the performing arts remains a powerhouse of ideas but is desperately underfunded; and there is no clear policy direction in dealing with the creative economy or managing the impacts of digital disruption on cultural industries. At the wider cultural level, the change of government in 2013 brought with it new perceptions of Australian cultural values that were affected partly by nostalgia for the sort of cultural attitudes of earlier conservative administrations, and partly by global developments in which many accepted cultural norms were challenged if not overthrown. In this period we saw increased conflict over a range of issues with cultural implications ranging from immigration to the treatment of Indigenous Australians.

So I conclude that the answer to my question today is essentially the same as it was a decade ago: thinking about cultural policy means reflecting on the nature of what Australian culture is, and in our constantly changing society this is a continuing necessity. Cultural policy doesn't have to be a document, the result of a formal process as it was in 1994 with *Creative Nation,* or again in 2013 with *Creative Australia.* It could be a more fluid and dynamic discussion, constantly re-invigorating debate and questioning the directions in which our cultural life was heading. So I am suggesting that, rather than another policy document at this time, we need to initiate a new and broadly based national conversation, an update, a re-think about who we are and where we are going.

In ideal circumstances *Creative Australia* would provide an excellent starting point for such a conversation. It is by no means a universally admired document, but the framework that it puts forward does provide an overview of the field that can be seen to rise above Party politics. Indeed its definitional proposition that

> *Australian culture is the embodiment of the distinctive values, traditions and beliefs that make being Australian in the 21st century unique—democratic, diverse, adaptive and grounded in one of the world's oldest living civilisations,*[59]

is one that is likely to be generally accepted, regardless of political leaning.

However, a proposal to start up a wide-ranging rumination on our culture and its values at this present time is most unlikely to appeal to the Prime Minister or his Cabinet, given the cultural conflicts that keep re-surfacing within the Coalition's own ranks, the Government's apparent lack of interest in the area, and its preoccupation with issues they would see as having higher priority. However, a debate about matters of relevance to a cultural policy does not have to be promoted by government. Indeed public discussion about all aspects of our culture and its values has a life of its own, and will continue without the need for government intervention.

Nevertheless, there must be some possibilities for government action in the cultural policy space. An alternative opportunity exists for some timely government action focused more narrowly on the arts, an area where policy has been subject to far too much uncertainty in recent years. The Minister for the Arts, Senator Mitch Fifield, has shown a keen interest in the arts sector and concern for its problems—perhaps he could be persuaded that to press the re-set button on arts policy would be a shrewd move on his part. He could initiate a fresh look at the present state of the creative arts in Australia, now that the assaults of the last few years have receded. It would be a way for him to further his engagement with the arts community, and enhance his own profile, with a relatively modest investment of public money to make it happen. In political terms, it would help him counter the common misperception that only the Labor and Green sides of politics support the arts.

He could do this by putting together a policy package of measures and announce them as setting some new directions for arts policy. They could be sold to the public as an initiative to improve the ways in which the Government and the Minister facilitate the production, distribution and consumption of the arts in Australia, to the benefit of communities across the length and breadth of the country. He will have his own ideas of what might be included, but here are some suggestions for components for a new arts policy package, derived from discussion in this paper:

- A recalibration and expansion of the artist-in-residence programs in schools;
- A forum or series of forums on arts funding, perhaps including a broad discussion of the role of peer assessment in evaluating grant applications;
- In conjunction with the Cultural Ministers' Statistics Working Group, persuade the ABS to re-establish the National Centre for Culture and Recreation Statistics;
- A program to increase funding for art centres in remote communities to enable expansion in their support for Aboriginal and Torres Strait Islander arts in all areas of art practice;

- Re-establishment of the Cultural Industries Innovation Centre;
- Set up a feasibility study to consider the establishment of a Heritage Lottery Fund.

So much for formal policy measures. At the same time the Minister could look to some simpler, more immediate and relatively inexpensive ideas that could reinvigorate public awareness and appreciation of the creative arts, and celebrate the ways in which engaging with the arts can lift our collective spirits. Some suggestions are: an open day/night in theatres, galleries, entertainment venues etc. across the country with free entry and top artists involved, including random appearances or performances by artists in public places such as shopping malls, city streets, etc. linked to an overall theme that art can be fun; a range of local programs in metropolitan and rural/regional cities and towns to get people/families engaged in creative activity—music, drama, writing, dance etc.; a Celebrate-the-Arts Day in Parliament House; provision of support for starting up Indigenous art fairs in some cities to complement those held in Darwin, Cairns and Adelaide; some surprising initiatives in international cultural/diplomatic relations, such as sending one of our major performing companies to North Korea; and an open day giving public access to historic government buildings.

Some of these suggestions may be quixotic, but they are all practical proposals for raising the national profile of the arts. They would complement the many existing activities such as festivals and public events and have a similar impact. For a small investment they could yield an immediate payoff in public engagement and cultural participation.

What of the longer term? If it is true that articulation of a more comprehensive cultural policy is unlikely to interest government at the present time, is there any prospect of this in the future? For instance, the next time the Labor Party wins office, the idea of a national cultural policy might well be return to the table. The new Minister could retrieve *Creative Australia* from the filing cabinet, dust it off, and consider how much of it would be still relevant five or six years on. Certainly Tony Burke, the Minister who took over briefly from Simon Crean, declared his full support for the document at the time. The Party might still feel the same way. If so, the new conversation about where we are and where we are going could take on a much more ambitious agenda.

Endnotes

All the digital references accessed by the author are still valid at the time of publication.

1 See James Curran, *The Power of Speech: Australian Prime Ministers Defining the National Image* (Melbourne: Melbourne University Press, 2004), Ch.6.

2 The *Platform Papers* series has seen some significant contributions to discussion of these issues. In the case of broadcasting, see Martin Harrison, *'Our ABC' A Dying Culture?*, Platform Papers 1, 2004; Kim Dalton, *Missing in Action: The ABC and Australia's Screen Culture*, Platform Papers 51, 2017. In the case of film, see Storry Walton, *Shooting Through: Australian Film and the Brain Drain*, Platform Papers 5, 2005; Lauren Carroll Harris, *Not at a Cinema Near You: Australia's Film Distribution Problem*, Platform Papers 37, 2013.

3 See David Throsby, *Does Australia Need a Cultural Policy?*, Platform Papers 7, 2006, pp. 46-47.

4 This section draws some of its ideas from my own writings about cultural policy, to which reference can be made for further detail; see particularly David Throsby, *The Economics of Cultural Policy*, (Cambridge: Cambridge University Press, 2010).

5 Jean Battersby, *Cultural Policy in Australia* (Paris: UNESCO, 1980).

6 For a discussion in an Australian context, see Katya Johanson, 'How Australian Industry Policy Shaped Cultural Policy' *International Journal of Cultural Policy* 14 (2008), pp. 139-48.

7 See Department for Culture Media and Sport UK. *Creative Industries Mapping Document 2001.* (London: DCMS, 2001); the original thirteen are now consolidated into nine: Advertising and marketing; Architecture; Crafts; Product, graphic and fashion design; Film, TV, video, radio and photography; IT, software and computer services; Publishing; Museums, galleries and libraries; and Music, performing and visual arts.

8 See UNCTAD, *Creative Economy Report,* (Geneva: United Nations, 2008, 2010); UNESCO/UNDP, *Creative Economy Report 2013 Special Edition,* (New York: United Nations Development Programme, 2013).

9 See Hristina Mikić, *Measuring the Economic Contribution of the Cultural Industries: A Review and Assessment of Current Methodological Approaches,* (Montreal: UNESCO Institute of Statistics, 2012).

10 Theodor Adorno and Max Horkheimer, *Dialektik der Aufklärung: Philosophische Fragmente,* (Amsterdam: Querido, 1947); English trans. by John Cumming, *Dialectic of Enlightenment,* (London: Verso, 1979).

11 David Throsby, 'The concentric circles model of the cultural industries', *Cultural Trends,* 17 (2008), pp. 147-64.

12 Department for Culture, Media and Sport, UK, *The Culture White Paper* (Cmnd 9218), (London: DCMS, 2016).

13 Much work has been undertaken by the National Endowment for Science, Technology and the Arts (Nesta) in

the UK in promoting the relevance of digital technologies in the cultural industries; see for example Nesta, *The Creative Economy, Arts and Culture*, (London: National Foundation for Science, Technology and the Arts, 2017).

14 The GREAT campaign is a cross-Government initiative designed to deliver trade and tourism benefits to the UK by harnessing the best that Britain has to offer under a single brand and promoting British strengths to the world; see further www.greatbritaincampaign.com

15 See *The Culture White Paper*, p. 44.

16 Australian Government, *Initial Summit Report: Australia 2020 Summit*, (Canberra: Department of the Prime Minister and Cabinet, 2008), p. 1.

17 *Initial Summit Report*, p. 29.

18 Australian Government, *Cultural Policy Discussion Paper*, (Canberra: Dept. of the Prime Minister and Cabinet, Office for the Arts, August 2011).

19 Stuart Cunningham, 'Where the Jobs Are: Why a National Cultural Policy Matters', *The Conversation*, 14 October, 2011. (https://theconversation.com/where-the-jobs-are-why-a-national-cultural-policy-matters-3430)

20 Ben Goldsmith, 'National Cultural Policy is Bold, but Vulnerable', *The Conversation*, 14 March, 2013, https://theconversation.com/national-cultural-policy-is-bold-but-vulnerable-12800

21 Michael Shmith, 'Giving Thanks to Creative Notions', *Sydney Morning Herald*, 16 March, 2013, http://www.smh.com.au/federal-politics/political-opinion/giving-thanks-to-creative-notions-20130315-2g5xw.html

22 See further in Josephine Caust, 'Cultural Wars in an

Australian Context: Challenges in Developing a National Cultural Policy' *International Journal of Cultural Policy* 21 (2015), pp. 168-82; for comment on the policy's recommendations on Indigenous arts, see Christine Judith Nicholls, 'Joining the Dots: Indigenous Art and Language in the National Cultural Policy', *The Conversation*, March 18, 2013 (https://theconversation.com/joining-the-dots-indigenous-art-and-language-in-the-national-cultural-policy-12806) and Jon Altman, 'Indigenous Cultural Policy: Creative Australia or Creative Accounting?' *The Conversation*, April 19, 2013. (https://theconversation.com/indigenous-cultural-policy-creative-australia-or-creative-accounting-13134)

23 See Lars Brandle, 'Australia's Arts Minister Simon Crean Out, "Creative Australia" Faces Unknown Fate', *Billboard*, 22 March 2013. (https://www.billboard.com/biz/articles/news/global/1554280/australias-arts-minister-simon-crean-out-creative-australia-faces)

24 Steve Dow, 'New Minister Stands by Arts Policy' *Sydney Morning Herald*, 25 March 2013. (https://www.smh.com.au/entertainment/new-minister-stands-by-arts-policy-20130325-2gpbj.html)

25 A recent example is in Susan Luckman. 'Cultural Policy and Creative Industries', in *The Routledge Handbook of Global Cultural Policy*, eds. Victoria Durrer, Toby Miller and Dave O'Brien, (Abingdon: Routledge, 2018), pp. 341-54.

26 Gabrielle Trainor and Angus James, *Review of the Australia Council*, (Canberra: Department of Regional Australia, Local Government, Arts and Sport, 2012); for some responses to the review, see Joyce Morgan, 'Culture of Excellence', *Sydney Morning Herald*, 19 May 2012; Esther

Anatolitis, 'We Need a Reimagined Australia Council', *Australian*, June 14, 2012. (https://www.theaustralian.com.au/archive/arts/we-need-a-reimagined-australia-council/news-story/5c90ead2f6fb10f36d431a44370f83f6)

27 Rupert Myer, 'New Investment in Australian Creativity', speech from the National Press Club, 13 March, 2013, http://www.australiacouncil.gov.au/news/media-centre/media-releases/new-investment-in-australian-creativity/

28 See, for example, Deborah Stone, 'Arts Leaders Protest Missing Freedoms [sic] in OzCo Act', *ArtsHub*, 9 April 2013. (http://www.artshub.com.au/news-article/features/arts/arts-leaders-protest-missing-freedoms-in-ozco-act-194935)

29 The Australia Council administers funding to the 28 major performing companies on behalf of the Australian Government and State governments under the so-called National Framework for Governments' Support of the Major Performing Arts Sector (the MPA Framework). The 28 companies are represented independently by an umbrella organisation, the Australian Major Performing Arts Group (AMPAG).

30 There was wide coverage of the boycott. See, for example, Alana Lentin and Javed de Costa, 'Sydney Biennale Boycott Victory Shows that Divestment Works', *Guardian*, 11 March 2014. (https://www.theguardian.com/commentisfree/2014/mar/11/sydney-biennale-boycott-victory-shows-that-divestment-works); and Andrew Taylor and Fiona Gruber, 'Biennale Boycott is the Latest in Long Line of Political Protests by Artists' *Sydney Morning Herald*, 15 March 2014. (https://www.smh.com.au/entertainment/art-and-design/biennale-boycott-is-the-latest-in-long-line-

of-political-protests-by-artists-20140314-34s0r.html). An overview of coverage of the boycott can be found at https://theconversation.com/au/topics/sydney-biennale-boycott-9340. For a wider view of artists' political protests, see Mel Evans, *Artwash: Big Oil and the Arts*, (London: Pluto Press, 2015).

31 For comments on this period, see for example, Justin O'Connor, 'Hockey's Budget Ignores the Cultural Economy, to its Shame', *The Conversation*, 15 May 2014, https://theconversation.com/hockeys-budget-ignores-the-cultural-economy-to-its-shame-26737; Steve Dow, 'State of the Arts: How the Abbott Government is Funding a High Culture War', *The Monthly* October 2014; Josephine Caust, 'Cultural Wars in an Australian Context: Challenges in Developing a National Cultural Policy', *International Journal of Cultural Policy*, 21:2 (2015), 168-82.

32 Quoted in John Gardiner-Garden, 'Arts and Film: Budget Review 2015–16 Index', https://www.aph.gov.au/About_Parliament/Parliamentary_Departments/Parliamentary_Library/pubs/rp/BudgetReview201516/Arts

33 See Ben Eltham and Deb Verhoeven, 'Philosophy vs Evidence is no Way to Orchestrate Cultural Policy', *The Conversation*, 28 September 2015, https://theconversation.com/philosophy-vs-evidence-is-no-way-to-orchestrate-cultural-policy-42487 (accessed 23 February 2018); Debbie Cuthbertson and Joel Meares, 'George Brandis Turns Arts into "Political Football" with $104.7m Australia Council Cuts', *Sydney Morning Herald*, 13 May 2015, http://www.smh.com.au/entertainment/art-and-design/george-brandis-turns-arts-into-political-football-with-1047m-australia-

council-cuts-20150512-gh0d0n.html; Alan Evans, 'Budget takes $100m from Australia Council to Establish Arts Excellence Program', *Guardian*, 13 May 2015, https://www.theguardian.com/australia-news/2015/may/12/budget-takes-100m-from-australia-council-to-establish-arts-excellence-program; and many more.

34 The events described in the following section are discussed more fully in David Throsby 'Commerce or Culture? Australian Book Industry Policy in the Twenty-first Century', in *Publishing Means Business: Australian Perspectives*, eds. Aaron Mannion, Millicent Weber and Katherine Day, (Clayton: Monash University Publishing, 2017), pp. 1-21.

35 Book Industry Strategy Group. *Final Report to Government*. (Canberra: Department of Innovation, Industry, Science and Research, 2011). p. 11.

36 Book Industry Collaborative Council. *Final Report*, (Canberra: Department of Industry, Innovation, Climate Change, Science, Research and Tertiary Education, 2013), p. 47.

37 Book Industry Collaborative Council 2013. *Final Report*, pp. 47-49.

38 Susan Wyndham, 'Government Give and Take to the Struggling Book Industry', *Sydney Morning Herald*, 16 December 2014. (https://www.smh.com.au/entertainment/books/government-give-and-take-to-the-struggling-book-industry-20141216-1288u1.html)

39 The formal announcement was made in the 2015 Mid-year Economic and Fiscal Outlook released the following day; see *Commonwealth of Australia, Mid-Year Economic*

and Fiscal Outlook 2015-16, (Canberra: Commonwealth of Australia, 2015) p. 152.

40 Alison Croggon, 'Black Friday: The Latest Round of Australia Council Funding is the Culmination of Years of Cuts and Mismanagement of Arts Funding', *The Monthly*, Blog, May 2016. (https://www.themonthly.com.au/blog/alison-croggon/2016/16/2016/1463358684/black-friday); Josephine Caust, 'The Continuing Saga around Arts Funding and the Cultural Wars in Australia', *International Journal of Cultural Policy*, 23 (2017), pp. 1-15.

41 Jo Caust, Joanna Mendelssohn, Julian Meyrick, Maria Miranda and Tully Barnett, 'Carnage in the Arts: Experts Respond to the Australia Council Cuts', *The Conversation,* May 13, 2016. (https://theconversation.com/carnage-in-the-arts-experts-respond-to-the-australia-council-cuts-59368); Wesley Enoch, 'Chaos in the Arts' *The Monthly*, July 2016. (https://www.themonthly.com.au/issue/2016/july/1467295200/wesley-enoch/chaos-arts); David Pledger, 'Friday Essay: Where to now for Australian Culture?' *The Conversation*, July 15, 2016. (https://theconversation.com/friday-essay-where-to-now-for-australian-culture-624390.

42 Matthew Westwood, 'Budget 2017-18: creating arts policy for growth', *Australian*, May 9, 2017. (https://www.theaustralian.com.au/budget-2017/budget-201718-creating-arts-policy-for-growth/news-story/f1908ebe8201e3954b6d451d94d1490a)

43 In 2015-16 total cultural funding by the Australian Government was $2,290 million, and by all levels of government it was $5,841 million; see *Commonwealth of Australia, Cultural Funding by Government, Australia, 2015–16,*

(Prepared by ABS for Meeting of Cultural Ministers, 2017).

44 See particularly Ben Eltham, *When the Goal Posts Move: Patronage, Power and Resistance in Australian Cultural Policy 2013-16,* Platform Papers 48, 2016.

45 For further discussion of the pursuit of excellence as a goal of arts policy, see Katharine Brisbane, *The Arts and the Common Good*, Platform Papers 43, May 2015.

46 For a discussion of the Australia Council in a broader context of Australian cultural policy, see Esther Anatolitis, 'Arts for Our Sake', *Meanjin*, Winter 2017. (https://meanjin.com.au/essays/arts-for-our-sake/).

47 See, for example, David Throsby and Ekaterina Petetskaya, *Integrating Art Production and Economic Development in the Kimberley: National Survey of Remote Aboriginal and Torres Strait Islander Artists*, Macquarie Economics Research Paper 2/2016, (Sydney: Macquarie University, 2016).

48 See Alice Woodhead and Tim Acker, The Art Economies Value Chain Reports: Synthesis. CRC-REP Research Report CROO4. (Alice Springs: Ninti One Limited, 3014.)

49 For an early assessment see Felicity Wright and Frances Morphy (eds.), *The Art and Craft Centre Story* (3 vols.), (Canberra: ATSIC, 1999-2000); a review of more recent literature can be found in Tim Acker, Lisa Stefanoff and Alice Woodhead, *Aboriginal and Torres Strait Islander Art Economies Project: Literature Review*. CRC-REP Working Paper CW010. (Alice Springs: Ninti One Ltd. 2013).

50 For an excellent outline of the implications of and

responses to the Statement, see Daniel McKay, *Uluru Statement: a Quick Guide*, (Parliamentary Library Research Paper Series 2016-17, Canberra, 19 June 2017).

51 There has been extensive discussion of this issue going back at least as far as Nugget Coombs' persuasive arguments in the 1970s; see H.C. Coombs, *Kulinma: Listening to Aboriginal Australians*, (Canberra: Australian National University Press, 1978) and later his *Aboriginal Autonomy: Issues and Strategies*, (Cambridge: Cambridge University Press, 1994). See also the proposal forcefully articulated in the outcome of the 2020 Summit in 2008.

52 The most recent is David Throsby and Katya Petetskaya, *Making Art Work: An Economic Study of Professional Artists in Australia*, (Sydney: Australia Council for the Arts, 2017).

53 Frank Moorhouse, 'Is Writing a Way of Life?' *Meanjin*, Autumn 2017. (https://meanjin.com.au/essays/is-writing-a-way-of-life/).

54 See further in Pierre-Michel Menger, *The Economics of Creativity: Art and Achievement under Uncertainty*, (Cambridge MA: Harvard University Press, 2014).

55 For a perspective on this issue, see Patrick Kabanda, 'The Creative Wealth of Nations: How the Performing Arts Can Advance Development and Human Progress', (*World Bank Policy Research Working Paper No. 7118*, (Washington DC: The World Bank, 2014) Available at SSRN: https://ssrn.com/abstract=2528316.

56 For contemporary coverage of responses to this event, see http://www.nytimes.com/2008/02/27/world/asia/27symphony.html?_r=1

57 *Productivity Commission, Conservation of Historic Heritage Places: Inquiry Report*, (Canberra: Productivity Commission, 2006).

58 The former CMC has been replaced by the Meeting of Cultural Ministers (MCM), which effectively serves the same purpose of bringing together the Commonwealth and State/Territory Arts Ministers and their corresponding bureaucrats for the purposes of coordinating their respective policies.

59 Quoted from *Creative Australia*, p. 27.

COPYRIGHT INFORMATION

PLATFORM PAPERS
Quarterly essays from Currency House Inc.
Founding Editor: Dr John Golder
Editor: Katharine Brisbane
Currency House Inc. is a non-profit association and resource centre advocating the role of the performing arts in public life by research, debate and publication.

Postal address: PO Box 2270, Strawberry Hills, NSW 2012, Australia
Email: info@currencyhouse.org.au Tel: (02) 9319 4953
Website: www.currencyhouse.org.au Fax: (02) 9319 3649

ISBN 978-0-9946130-8-0
ISSN 1449-583X

Typeset in Garamond
Printed by Ligare Book Printers, Riverwood, NSW
Production by Currency Press Pty Ltd

FORTHCOMING

PP No.56, August 2018

FALLING THROUGH THE GAPS:
Our performers' health and welfare
Mark R W Williams

Many health and welfare professionals are sincere advocates for the role of arts in promoting mental health and wellbeing in the wider population; but other studies are showing that among professional artists and crews the level of mental ill-health, suicidal ideation and suicide is up to ten times that of the general Australian population. US studies show life expectancy in pop musicians could be thirty years shorter. This paper examines the factors that shorten the lives and diminish the wellbeing of workers in the performing arts. Economists have argued that psychic reward in the arts is legitimately quite different from that of pecuniary reward. But in reality, there are other problems: residual income, length of engagements, decentred work, welfare benefits, superannuation and housing. The consequences will soon overtake another generation. If we are to have a strong performing arts culture, we need to prevent performing artists falling through the gaps.